The Manipulator

Morne Fourie's Personal Insight Series, Volume 1

Morne Fourie

Published by Morne Fourie, 2025.

THE MANIPULATOR

First edition. October 11, 2025.

ISBN: 978-1037097393

Written by Morne Fourie.

Table of Contents

THE
MANIPULATOR
A personal insight and guide for
vegetarian wolves
MORNE FOURIE

Morne Fourie

The Manipulator

A personal insight and guide for vegetarian wolves.

ISBN: 978-1-0370-9739-3

Preface

This document does not stem from the hallowed halls of academia, nor does it seek refuge in scholarly discourse. Rather, it is the fruit of experience, an accumulation of moments, observations, and revelations that have shaped my understanding of the world and the people within it. I have arrived at a juncture in my existence where introspection is not merely a passing indulgence but a necessity, an opportunity to examine myself in the grand tapestry of context. Context within my environment, and more profoundly, context in relation to the intricate web of human interactions.

I trust that some of you will find resonance in my reflections, perhaps wisdom from my journey. At the very least, I hope to offer a window through which you might view your own existence with fresh perspective, a vantage point that sparks contemplation, self-awareness, and, should it serve you well, meaningful application in your own life.

Let me be unequivocal, I am not a psychologist, nor do I claim mastery over the complexities of the human mind. However, driven by an insatiable curiosity and a desire to understand both myself and those around me, I have delved into the literature of human behaviour, seeking patterns, motivations, and underlying truths. My life's path has been paved with the trials and triumphs of business and corporate engagement, where success is often dictated not solely by strategy, but by the delicate art of human understanding. Whether among colleagues, superiors, subordinates, employees, suppliers, or customers, I have come to the realization, that beyond titles and transactions, we are all, at our core, simply people. And to truly navigate the intricacies of professional and personal relationships, one must first master the art of comprehension. Comprehending, dissecting and understanding the driving forces that propel individuals, discerning their motives, and, most critically, recognizing the methods by which we exert influence upon the world and those around us.

Take this understanding and wield it wisely. Apply it in your workplace, in the ventures you pursue, in the bonds you forge in love and friendship, and, perhaps most crucially, in the guidance you offer to your children. The ability to grasp the nuances of human behaviour is not merely a tool but a profound gift, one that, when used with wisdom and integrity, can illuminate paths previously shrouded in uncertainty. My hope is that you find value in this perspective and come to recognize the undeniable utility of truly understanding the people who inhabit your world.

We all manipulate

"Rubbish! I don't manipulate." I hear your protest already. But bear with me, I use the term manipulation quite deliberately. While I will explore its definition and distinguish it from influence more thoroughly in the second chapter, for now, I ask that you suspend judgment and consider the premise I lay before you.

From the moment we take our first breath, we instinctively begin to shape and command our surroundings, wielding influence upon those who tend to our needs. Infants, fragile yet relentless, master the art of manipulation before they have even grasped language or logic. When hunger gnaws at their tiny frames, they do not reason, they do not request, they cry, piercing the air with raw distress. That singular act holds power, compelling their mother or caregiver to respond, to satisfy their need. But hunger is not their only driver. Studies have shown that infants cry not only for nourishment but also for attention, learning, perhaps subconsciously, that their cries evoke a reaction. This simple act of cause and effect sets the foundation for a lifetime of social interplay.

Psychologists debate the extent to which infants consciously manipulate. Some argue that even at fifteen months, a child can exhibit behaviours designed to influence caregivers, crying not out of necessity, but to summon attention. Others claim that such intent requires cognitive complexity beyond the reach of a young mind, suggesting that infants merely respond to emotional distress rather than engaging in calculated manipulation.

And therein lies the heart of my argument. We do not always manipulate intentionally. Much of our influence over others is driven by subconscious desires, guiding our actions in ways we may not even recognize.

Consider the toddler who intervenes in moments of parental affection. A father reaches for his partner's hand, a gesture of closeness and warmth. But suddenly, the child interjects. Arms flailing in protest, declaring ownership over their mother: "My mommy!" They push away the father's embrace, inserting themselves between the couple as if reclaiming territory. And yet, when the parents sit apart, void of affection, there is no objection from the child. Why? Because the child perceives a shift, a change in dynamics that, whether consciously or not, they feel compelled to restore to their own advantage.

This instinctual interplay stretches beyond mere behaviour. It is deeply biological. Babies under the age of three can detect the pheromones released by their parents, further reinforcing the invisible thread of attachment and connection. Research suggests that this bond begins even before birth; while still in the womb, a foetus becomes attuned to their mother's pheromones, aiding in post-birth recognition. Breastfeeding strengthens this intimate tie, with new-borns able to distinguish their mother's scent within mere days. These chemical cues serve as silent guides, helping infants seek comfort, nourishment, and security in the arms they trust most.

From infancy to adulthood, we learn, adapt, and refine the ways in which we interact with and influence the world around us. Sometimes consciously, sometimes instinctively, but always, manipulation remains part of the human experience.

Instinct, Survival, and the Genesis of Manipulation

The child's impulse to interfere is not driven by simple curiosity or momentary jealousy. It is deeply rooted in survival. A primal, prehistoric instinct awakens at the first hint of competition for mommy's attention. Affection between parents signals the potential for repeated procreation, which, in the child's undeveloped yet ferociously perceptive mind, translates to an existential threat. Another sibling would mean divided resources, food, care, and love. Forcing the child to compete for sustenance and significance. And so, the child moves pre-emptively, asserting dominance before the threat materializes.

Perhaps this instinct is triggered by the pheromones released between parents during moments of intimacy, an invisible cue perceived beyond conscious thought. Or perhaps it is a simple visual reaction. The sight of daddy encroaching upon the sacred space that, in the child's view, is meant for them alone. Regardless of the source, what follows is swift and decisive action. Intervention. The child cannot tolerate the dilution of its exclusivity, cannot abide the intrusion into mommy's affectionate embrace. Whether through verbal protest, physical obstruction, or even forceful resistance, by crying, clawing, pushing away, the child asserts itself.

Children, unable to articulate complex emotions, often resort to primal expressions of frustration. And here, jealousy emerges. Not as a learned trait, but as an instinctual force. A child's developing social awareness is still crude, still evolving, yet the subconscious drive to manipulate circumstances in their favour is undeniable.

A study from Nurture Infant House explores this phenomenon, noting how toddlers often become visibly upset when parents engage in affectionate exchanges. The child, attached more deeply to one parent, struggles with the notion of sharing that bond. Duke University Medical

School reinforces this idea, finding that parental warmth and attention serve as foundational elements in emotional development. Children who receive affectionate engagement tend to grow into individuals with greater emotional stability. They are less anxious, more secure.

But in the immediate moment, none of this concerns the child. What matters is victory. If daddy concedes, if he withdraws from the embrace, the child has won. And in that triumph, the child tastes power.

Power to manipulate. Power to control. Power to bend the environment and even mommy and daddy, to their will.

Regardless of whether this dominance serves the child's long-term well-being, the immediate gratification is intoxicating. And as with all learned behaviours, reinforcement breeds repetition. The next time an opportunity arises, the child will act again. If the parents once more acquiesce, if they reinforce this pattern, the child recognizes its emerging authority. The realization dawns, whether consciously or instinctively:

"If I want things to go my way, I possess the ability and means to manipulate others, even my own caregivers, into submission."

This is an extraordinary level of power for a small child to wield. A child who has not yet grasped the concept of sharing, who does not yet comprehend the true value of parental unity. A child whose tunnel vision permits only selfish impulses, dismissing the larger reality that a strong parental bond benefits them in ways they cannot yet fathom. But foresight is not a trait of infancy, rather short-term desire reigns supreme.

Thus, the child refines their craft, sharpening their manipulative instincts. And soon, with growing confidence, they begin to expand the reach of their control.

The Birth of Entitlement

A simple excursion to the shop, a seemingly ordinary moment, becomes a battlefield of wills. The child's desire is clear, immediate, and unwavering. A sweet. A simple, tantalizing indulgence. But the mother, guided by reason, deems the request ill-timed or undesirable and utters the dreaded denial. No.

For a fleeting moment, the child considers the weight of that word. But then, instinct overrides reason. It is time to escalate. To refine and expand the utility of manipulation. The protest begins, not with words, but with an explosion of limbs and sound. A visceral display of defiance. Screaming. Kicking. The small body trembles with indignation, a storm of raw demand unleashed.

Mommy looks around. The child watches, sensing vulnerability, reading the cues with uncanny precision. Embarrassment. Hesitation. A crack in the armour. Encouraged, the child redoubles its efforts, heightening the spectacle, intensifying the assault. If mere protest did not suffice, then surely relentless fury will.

"Thou shalt yield to my desire, mother."

Too often, parents relent. Whether from exhaustion, a lack of conviction, or the sheer desperation for peace and quiet, they surrender. And in that moment, something profound occurs, the manipulative behaviour is not merely reinforced, but rewarded. A precedent is set.

We condone what we tolerate.

The child, victorious, makes a mental note, a lesson carved into their developing mind for future use. Mother has condoned my tantrum. She has granted my wish. And so, as the battle dies down, the spoils are claimed, a sweet earned through sheer perseverance. A triumph of manipulation, proof that with enough force, the world can be bent to personal desire.

But as the mother resumes her shopping, relieved to finally focus on the task at hand, she remains blissfully unaware of the beast she has nurtured. The demon child, the one parents whisper about in hushed tones, the spoiled tyrant who commands authority not through merit, but through sheer, unrelenting demand.

She has unknowingly planted the seed of self-centred entitlement. A cost far greater than the price of a single sweet.

A stronger approach, a firm NO, followed by fleeting tears and eventual acceptance, could have preserved the balance. After all, children are easily distracted, their whims fleeting, their grievances short-lived. But in choosing appeasement, she has unwittingly forged her role. No longer the guiding authority, but the servant. At the beck and call of her child's desire, yielding whenever the storm of protest looms.

My father had a phrase for this, I recall. "Obedient and well-behaved parents." Instead of raising obedient and well-behaved children, parents become subjects of the child's expanding dominion.

Jordan Peterson captured this fundamental principle in Twelve Rules for Life: "The purpose of the parents is to raise the child in a way that renders the child socially acceptable."

But what happens when boundaries are continuously tested, stretched, and discarded? The spoiled, entitled brat emerges. The product of the devouring mother, a figure who unconsciously suffocates the child's need for independence. In her relentless pursuit to please, she forfeits her authority, rebuilding the umbilical tether, binding them together beyond necessity, beyond reason.

The result? A socially unacceptable child, rejected by a world that does not operate on indulgence. And a mother unable, or unwilling, to let go, to allow the child to evolve beyond dependency. Both have played their roles in this elaborate dance of manipulation, each selfish in their own right.

The entitled child, groomed for a world that, in truth, owes it nothing.

To borrow the words of Barry Naude in his book Don't BS Yourself: "Life is not a fairy-tale without villains. This is a tough world filled with obstacles, traps, and villains. These obstacles, traps, and villains are life's realities and challenges that we all experience throughout our life."

And when the entitled child finally steps into this world, unprepared, unequipped, the harsh reality will strike with merciless precision.

Entitlement and the Consequences of a Manipulated World

Life presents us with obstacles, challenges that demand resilience, discipline, and the ability to adapt. To rise above mediocrity, we must cultivate these skills, equipping ourselves to navigate a complex and often unforgiving world. Yet, when parents relinquish their authority in favour of appeasement, they unwittingly rob their children of the ability to fend for themselves.

Then we wonder, why do we find ourselves surrounded by entitled, self-centred individuals? Adults clinging to dependency, stagnating in their parents' basements, unwilling or unable to claim responsibility for their own existence. Societal deviants indulging in peculiar excesses, unmoored from reality, driven by delusions that defy both science and reason. The normalization of concepts once considered absurd, where biology and language are treated as malleable constructs, dictated not by truth but by personal desire.

And when society refuses to bend, when recognition is denied, the response is predictable, outrage, victimhood, and retaliation. Some intentionally create opportunities to ensnare others, to bait them into so-called transgressions. The act of "misgendering" becomes a weapon, a calculated manoeuvre designed not for discourse, but for condemnation. The public spectacle unfolds much like the tantrum in the shopping aisle, a relentless demand for compliance, fuelled not by genuine grievance, but by a manipulative pursuit of control.

There is a moment when the thought arises, a common sentiment among those who value discipline: "All that child needs is a firm correction to set them straight." Not harm, not cruelty, but clear, unwavering boundaries. A refusal to indulge the whims of manipulation. For tolerating such behaviour, whether in children or adults, only reinforces it, expanding its reach until it infects entire social structures.

The truth is, we all possess the right to opinion and personal identity. If someone chooses to identify as a pot plant, so be it. But the expectation that society must validate and accommodate every individual whim is where the line must be drawn. Freedom does not extend to the forced manipulation of others, no one has the right to demand participation in their illusions, nor to wield outrage as a tool for coercion.

And so, the cycle of manipulation continues, refined, expanded, entrenched into society. Unless we recognize it, confront it, and refuse to yield to its demands.

Naturally, those that confront such notions are criticized and considered insensitive and cruel. I expect criticism for my opinion in this very volume. However, we need to ask ourselves: what is worst, speaking the truth, or hurting someone's feelings. Truth, in my opinion, is far more valuable and constructive, than amicability. It is required. Necessary.

The Thin Line Between Influence and Manipulation

Influence and manipulation, two sides of the same coin, indistinguishable at times except for the intent behind them. Both are tools wielded in the shaping of our world, subtle forces that guide behaviours, decisions, and outcomes.

We influence constantly. With purpose, with habit, with necessity. The way our employees carry out their tasks. The materials our children use to cover their books. The time we set for dinner, the rituals of a Sunday afternoon. We dictate fashion norms, behavioural expectations, even the cadence of conversations, all through commentary, critique, and silent insistence. We protest what unsettles us, mock what we disapprove of. Through repetition, we mould the world to suit our preferences, for better or worse.

For the individual, the 'I' is always right, until proven otherwise.

But the line is crossed when influence turns inward, when its purpose is no longer communal but self-serving. Influence becomes manipulation when its motive is driven by personal gain. When the desired outcome serves only the self, without regard for the well-being or autonomy of others.

You might argue, "But I have no malicious intent when influencing, so how can it be called manipulation?" A fair question. Yet, intent is rarely pure. More often than not, our drive is rooted in self-interest, even when concealed under layers of justification. We influence because it benefits us, because it shapes our world into something that aligns with our desires. And in that pursuit, manipulation becomes the unspoken language of control.

We manipulate our surroundings, defining space and structure, arranging furniture, choosing the colour of the drapes, deciding where each tool must hang in the garage. We tweak processes and refine appearances, all in the service of crafting an environment that feels right, that fosters comfort, efficiency, and a sense of ownership. But at its core, the direction we continuously shape is determined by our own preferences alone.

Then, there is the restless few of us, whom always seek better. Perfection remains elusive; contentment is fleeting. We scrutinize, critique, and reimagine endlessly. We adjust, refine, and elevate, never settling, never satisfied. This drive, the unrelenting thirst for progress, manifests itself as continuous manipulation. Of environments. Of processes. Of relationships. The shape of our world bends under this force, shifting to accommodate the vision we relentlessly pursue. Don't get me wrong, ambition drives progress. And this is very admirable in a career. However, when it comes to relationship, it is counterproductive. Never being satisfied with what you have and always seeking better, will most certainly render one lonely and deserted. And yes, I am speaking through experience. Seeking improvement WITHIN a relationship is good. Enrichment of the bond will strengthen and cement it. But seeking improvement OUTSIDE of the relationship, seeking a 'better partner' or 'better' relationship, more often than not results in a lonely, microwave dinner for one.

Ambition, growth, and societal expectation demand change, and change demands influence. Yet, where influence thrives, manipulation lurks in the shadows, waiting for opportunity. A strategy disguised as necessity, justified under the pursuit of excellence. And so, the cycle continues, whether we acknowledge it or not.

Manipulation: The Survival Mechanism of a Competitive World

Psychologists suggest that manipulation is often an adaptive trait, born from survival instincts, learned behaviours, and social conditioning. Psychology Today notes that chronic manipulation often stems from complex family dynamics, socio-economic disadvantages, or professional environments where cunning tactics are not only tolerated but rewarded. Some individuals develop manipulative tendencies as a necessary tool for navigating power struggles, shaping circumstances, or exerting influence where direct approaches are ineffective, or outright impossible.

Additionally, Verywell Mind highlights that manipulation operates on both conscious and subconscious levels. It is frequently used to control situations or people for personal advantage, reinforced by societal norms that favour strategic persuasion over brute force. Civilization may have veered away from physical conquest, but the hunger for control remains undiminished, merely reshaped, repackaged, and refined.

Now, imagine for a moment that you are a god-like entity, peering through a celestial microscope at the sprawling, teeming expanse of humanity. Billions of tiny organisms, individuals, scurrying within their confined habitats, each engaged in a relentless effort to manipulate their surroundings and those within them, moulding reality into something they deem acceptable. The world is a battlefield, not of swords and warriors, but of subtle influence, calculated persuasion, and the quiet assertion of control.

As civilization evolved, raw force became socially unacceptable. No longer could one raise a crusade, don armour, and strike down all opposition without consequence. And so, strategy replaced steel. Diplomacy became weaponized, and manipulation emerged as the more refined method of domination, silent, insidious, and infinitely more effective.

We erect rules, norms, laws, and when those prove insufficient, by-laws. More control. More regulation. More avenues through which manipulation can flourish under the guise of order. One of the most striking examples of this modern-day control mechanism? The dreaded Homeowners' Association (HOA), an abominable breeding ground for bureaucracy, rigid enforcement, and the self-righteous crusaders of conformity.

A perfect stage for the Karens of the world. Those who thrive on wielding authority well beyond their mandate, manipulating everyone and everything to suit their meticulously curated preferences. The HOA gives them the illusion of legitimized dominance, allowing them to dictate the minutiae of personal property. What colour gutters may be painted, what lawn ornaments are permissible, which plants offend the aesthetic purity of the neighbourhood. It matters not that the homeowner owns the property, has laboured for it, has earned it, because within the iron grip of an HOA, ownership becomes a conditional privilege, granted under the watchful eyes of those who seek control.

And herein lies the lesson, the extent to which people will go, their relentless pursuit of influence, their unwavering desire to shape, mould, and manipulate everything around them. From individual interactions to sprawling societal structures, the machinery of control runs ever forward, sustained by the quiet, subtle, and often unnoticed mechanics of manipulation.

Why We Manipulate

Manipulation is not merely an occasional tactic, it is an intrinsic part of human behaviour, woven into our struggle for survival. It is a means of adapting, influencing, and asserting control over our environment. And once the basic necessities of existence are secured, manipulation does not cease; rather, it refines itself, evolving as we climb the rungs of Maslow's Hierarchy of Needs, shifting from survival instincts to the pursuit of esteem, belonging, and self-actualization.

One of the earliest lessons in manipulation stems from childhood, when individuals first grasp the importance of control in uncertain and competitive environments. Consider the school setting, crowded classrooms, social hierarchies, and the relentless struggle to excel and stand out. The rules of engagement are unspoken but universally understood: adapt or be overlooked. The process of integration follows a predictable cycle: norm, form, storm.

First, we norm, we conform to social standards, blending into the broader collective out of fear of isolation. We like what others like, speak as they speak, act as they act. Then, within that broad spectrum, we form by gravitating toward subgroups that reflect shared interests, values, and ideals. Finally, some seek to storm to rebel, to excel, to rise above, distinguishing themselves within their chosen subgroup as unique, exceptional, a force to be reckoned with.

And very often, manipulation plays a key role in achieving this distinction.

Consider the bully, the self-proclaimed ruler of the social hierarchy. They do not simply emerge, they assert themselves, leveraging manipulation and intimidation to command authority. They wield fear as a tool, ensuring compliance through calculated influence.

Which brings us to the next motive: power and control.

Some manipulate not merely for survival, but for dominion. To hold sway over others, to shape interactions, decisions, and outcomes in their favour. We call it bullying in childhood, and leadership or strategy in adulthood, but the mechanisms remain eerily similar.

Parents lament when their child is bullied, yet once that child steps into the adult world, there is no protective buffer. The rules have changed, brutally so. The child who has never learned to navigate conflict, who has never faced adversaries, walks into reality utterly unprepared. They assume fairness, expect civility, believe the world will accommodate them. Only to be met with a harsh and indifferent system, where profit and competition reign supreme.

What follows is the slow unravelling, a person adrift, defeated, unable to find fulfilment in a relentless, unforgiving world. The potential fades, swallowed by failure, buried beneath regret. And in this bleak reckoning, there remains only one refuge, to retreat, to cling to the familiar, to run back to the safety of mommy's apron strings. If they are fortunate enough to still have a mother willing to take them in. Because out here, there are no second chances, only survival.

Survival of the Fittest: Nature's Brutal Reality

Consider for a moment the way nature governs itself. Take puppies, for example. Barely moments after birth, they begin their journey. Blind, fragile, yet instinctively driven. Soon, mobility arrives, and with it, the ritual of play: barking, growling, mock fights. These seemingly innocent interactions are far more than mere entertainment, they are the earliest lessons in survival. The puppy learns how to be a dog. How to bite, how to fight, how to hunt. Before domestication, such skills determined survival; they were not optional, but fundamental.

Dogs, after all, are pack animals. They do not thrive in isolation but within structured hierarchies, where dominance dictates order. Strength, not necessarily size, determines leadership, and thus, even in infancy, the battle for position begins. Sibling rivalries unfold, dominance is asserted, and inevitably, the runt of the litter suffers. The weakest among them will face relentless bullying. Last to suckle, last to feed, reminded of their low rank by the sharp bite of a more dominant sibling.

This is nature's way, an unflinching adherence to survival of the fittest. The strong endure, the weak falter. Nature does not extend kindness, nor does it offer sanctuary for frailty. The runt must adapt or perish, securing the bloodline's strength by ensuring only the most resilient genes persist. Brutal though it may seem, it is necessary. An organic process that defines survival itself.

And yet, in contrast to the animal kingdom, modern human society has softened. Human rights, equality, equity and consideration has taken the place of the natural order of things. Conflict among children, once an organic means of forging resilience, has been systematically erased, dismissed as cruel and unnecessary. In our attempt to shelter and protect, we have inadvertently created a false reality, one in which children grow up oblivious to struggle, untouched by the very adversity that would have made them strong. For the strong protect the weak, but if the strong is weakened for the sake of the lesser to feel better, whom will be there to protect?

Participation trophies and the obsessive safeguarding of emotions have dismantled primal structures once used to determine strength and hierarchy. But adulthood is not, contrary to the wishful thinking of some, a fair game. There are no consolation prizes in life, no equal distribution of success, no second-place awards in job interviews. You win, or you lose. You have, or you have not. You adapt, or you fail. Try harder, or accept your position.

The harsh taste of failure, introduced early, forces children to push harder, to earn what they seek, to fight their way up the hierarchy, equipping them with the emotional resilience necessary to thrive as adults. Yet, when shielded from reality, the moment they finally encounter the world's cold truth, they recoil, not in strength, but in protest. They claim unfairness, bigotry, prejudice. I am not as special as I was told. I am, in fact, average.

And for some, that realization sparks a desperate bid to change the playing field. If mediocrity defines them in one arena, why not redefine the arena itself? Shift the parameters, rewrite the rules. Perhaps, in a different category, they will be stronger. Perhaps then, victory can be achieved.

And if recognition is still denied? Claim victimhood. Accuse the world of oppression. Demand compliance. If that doesn't work, threaten suicide. The same tantrum thrown in childhood, now repurposed for adulthood.

Society cannot shield its children forever. Eventually, the real world arrives, and when it does, only those prepared for its trials will rise above its challenges.

The Importance of Balance in Discipline

At this point, I feel it necessary to emphasize a critical caution: while discipline is vital, extremes must be avoided. Neither unchecked leniency nor oppressive strictness serve a child's development well. True guidance requires balance, a delicate interplay between love and structure, nurture and consequence.

Children need love and attention. They need to understand the purpose of rules, why they exist, how to abide by them, and the consequences of breaking them. This balance, however, is elusive, requiring constant reassessment and wisdom. Parenting is no simple feat; it is a lifelong craft, refined through experience, error, and adaptation.

I speak from personal reflection. My father, a man I deeply respect and will always remember, was not always my hero. As the youngest of three brothers, I watched my eldest sibling struggle under my father's firm and dominant rule. I recall instances where corporal punishment was administered not because I had done wrong, but because my father believed that if one child erred, all should bear the consequence.

My eldest brother rebelled, defied authority, and we all suffered for it. I harboured resentment toward him and fear for my father. Yet, with time, perhaps through my mother's quiet protest or the humbling wake-up call of my father's first heart attack at forty-two, his approach shifted. Strict discipline gave way to understanding; punishment was coupled with explanation. Some might argue that I am a product of his later, more balanced years.

Regardless, my eldest brother never found stability. He struggled to hold onto employment, fractured relationships, and lacked both discipline and self-control. I loved him, despite his failings. In the end, he spent his final years under my parents' roof. Ill, penniless, and ostracized by his own children and friends. His life was a testament to the dangers of unchecked rebellion and unresolved discipline.

As a parent, I strive to avoid the tyranny I once knew. I approach discipline not with immediacy, but with evaluation, weighing the situation before acting.

A recent example stands out. My youngest daughter confided in me about her attempt to skip school. Her mother had already learned of the incident, delivered a stern lecture, and insisted she tell me herself. I watched as she nervously rubbed her palms together, her gaze darting away, avoiding eye contact. It was clear, the weight of her mistake had already settled upon her. There was little point in administering further punishment. Instead, I asked, "Did you learn your lesson?" She nodded. Yes. "And what have you learned?" She dutifully replied, "Rules exist for a reason..." (Here, I humorously interject that she wouldn't dare say "blah blah blah" to me, I've added that for brevity.) Satisfied with her understanding, I offered one final lesson: "If you ever decide to skip school again, at least don't get caught doing it."

Her mother protested playfully, but the message was clear, actions have consequences, and repetition will be met with greater severity.

The Many Faces of Manipulation

Manipulation, at its core, is often rooted in emotional insecurity. Those who struggle with a fractured sense of self-worth may wield manipulation as a tool, whether consciously or subconsciously, to validate their emotions or shield themselves from rejection. Rather than confronting their vulnerabilities, they may redirect attention, distort narratives, or undermine others, all in an effort to elevate themselves. Gossip, ridicule, calculated persuasion, it all serves a singular purpose: self-preservation through control.

Beyond individual psychology, external forces contribute to the normalization of manipulative behaviour. In certain cultures, and professions, strategic persuasion is not merely encouraged, it is an art form, a necessary skill for survival. Competitive industries demand sharp minds, calculated movements, and the ability to outmanoeuvre rivals. In warfare, business, and politics, manipulation often parades as strategy, indistinguishable from the logic of victory itself.

History offers no shortage of examples. The Spartans, shaped by an unforgiving society, thrived within a rigid hierarchy where tactical prowess was paramount. In Japan, the most prestigious military title was not that of warrior or general, but strategist, a role that emphasized intellect over brute force. Even today, corporate leaders turn to ancient texts like The Art of War by Sun Tzu and The Prince by Machiavelli, seeking wisdom on cunning, psychological warfare, and the mastery of influence.

And then, of course, there is personality. Some individuals possess traits that lend themselves more naturally to manipulation, whether through charm, ambition, or profound emotional intelligence. Psychological assessments like the Myers-Briggs Type Indicator (MBTI) suggest that certain types, driven by strategy or introspection, may be more prone to subtle or overt manipulation:

ENTP – The Debater: the quick-witted and endlessly persuasive, individuals. They may use their intellect and charisma to steer situations in their favour.

ENTJ – The Commander: Bold, ambitious, and strategic people. ENTJs often use calculated influence to achieve their goals, regardless of opposition. Resistance is futile after all.

INFJ – The Advocate: Typically, empathetic people, but capable of leveraging emotional intelligence to subtly manipulate the emotions and decisions of others. Often using guilt, fear or the puppy-dog eyes, or fluttering eyelids technique.

INTJ – The Mastermind: Visionary and methodical individuals. INTJs may orchestrate circumstances to fit their long-term objectives, sometimes with surgical precision. They take their time and often you don't see the manipulation coming. Let's take over the world, Pinkie!

Manipulation serves a range of motives, wealth, power, influence, acceptance, survival. Whether driven by ambition, fear, or self-indulgence, the instinct remains the same: control over one's reality, by any means necessary.

There is not one personality that exclusively can be classified as manipulators. As we have seen, we all manipulate to some extent or another. Take care not to classify someone as such without careful consideration. I highlight these personality types as typical, since these individuals are driven by a certain desire and possess the means to achieve it.

Not all manipulation is one-on-one. Manipulation takes on many faces. Society is riddled with systemic manipulation. From political parties to churches. Modern-day businesses utilize sophisticated algorithms and complex systems to gather data and to steer markets.

Social media has evolved into a tool of manipulation. Marketing is nothing less than influencing people to prefer one product over another. One narrative over another. The product, oh the product. It has evolved too. The focus has shifted from mere consumables, to include loyalty, support and subscription.

Politicians thrive on the support of numbers. Poles are nothing more than a body-count. So, they prey on the ignorant, selling exactly what the ignorant want. Promising them "freedom", hardly ever delivering. Politicians sell lies, manipulating truth and omitting important details, all in an effort to accumulate numbers. Then in order to stay at the top of the political hierarchy, they institute laws, acts, regulations, social grants and more, to make society dependant on the state. Nothing more than modern-day slavery.

The monetization of faith is nothing new. The Catholic church sold indulgences to raise funds to build lavish cathedrals and fund the church's expansion. Indulgences were pieces of paper sold in the market. Peasants would spend their life savings, handing it over to the priest, that would in turn write the name of a deceased loved one on the paper, guaranteeing passage to heaven. Commoditizing religion, salvation itself. The rise of the Protestant movement sought to undo the injustices brought upon the people by the Catholic church. Only to become commercialized and corrupted, itself. Today, there are hardly any churches that do not thrive on money and wealth. Religion has shifted from the spiritual wellness of devout souls, to stroking the egos of the willing. Preachers, selectively selling whatever makes people feel good about themselves, as long as they open their wallets and humbly pay their tithes.

Now, I have no illusions about churches needing money to function. I simply have a fundamental issue the funds finding their way into the pockets of the preachers and church leaders. But when church leaders fly around in private helicopters, live in lavish estates and wear expensive brands, the purpose of religion and the role of the church is corrupted. The so-called church becomes the very evil it is supposed to oppose. Such is the power of manipulation. The ability to use something pure, sacred, for personal gain. Selfish. Self-centred.

Systemic manipulation uses the very techniques exposed in the experiments. People's fear of standing out. Being different. Opposing the masses. People flock and herd. More often than not, they are no different. Sheep.

A farmer in the southern regions of Scotland, divided his grazing fields into two, with a fence. In the middle of the fence, he positioned a gate. The sheep would graze one half, until it was depleted. Then the farmer would have them graze the other half. When the farmer passed, his son took over the farm. He decided to remove the fence. However, he left the posts and the gate in the middle of the field.

When the sheep were let out in the morning to graze, they would first deplete the one section, never progressing past the line where the fence used to be. And when the farmer opened the fenceless gate, the sheep would rush and bottleneck at the gate, eager to get through to the lush grazing fields. Never crossing where the fence used to be.

This is typical of sheep. Typical of humans too. We herd. We bottleneck and queue to follow the masses. Not daring to be different. And we do it at the cost of our conscience. Knowing the difference between right and wrong. Yet we follow blindly. Voting for those whom we know won't deliver. We pray in the halls of, no longer cathedrals, but mall-like structures, built to accommodate the masses.

People blindly follow manipulators. Whether they stand on podiums with a neatly trimmed moustache, or perhaps wearing a red militant barrette, waving a first in the air, screaming liberation. Or a fish-shaped hat, carving religious symbols in the air with bloodstained fingers and a reverent expression. It is all the product of systemic manipulation.

Evaluate, scrutinise and look past the rhetoric. Dare to be different and to stand up for what you believe in. Even if it means you having to swim upstream. Against the current.

Manipulation and the Chemistry of Dominance

The life of a dog, like that of its ancestral counterpart, the wolf, is governed by structure. Within a pack, roles are defined with precise order: the alpha, responsible for leadership and decision-making; the protectors, ensuring the safety of the group; the caretakers, who maintain harmony; and the rest, who occupy the lower tiers of the hierarchy.

But that hierarchy is never static. The alpha, the ruling force, must defend his position, for younger, testosterone-fuelled challengers will inevitably rise, seeking to overthrow the patriarch through sheer physical power. Dominance is not granted, it is fought for, earned, and continually maintained.

Domesticated dogs carry these instincts within them. Where two or more dogs coexist, they form an internal pack, and this pack includes their human owners. But not all owners are recognized as alphas. Disobedient dogs reject human authority because, in their minds, the hierarchy is still unresolved. For a dog to truly submit, it must acknowledge dominance, not merely obey commands.

Within any canine group, position matters. You can visualize it as a ladder, each member occupying a step, constantly manoeuvring for higher ground. Those lower on the ladder seek to ascend, while those at the top must fight, whether through sheer force or subtle strategy, to remain in power.

A friend of mine once unknowingly cultivated such a hierarchy. He owned a mixed pack of dogs, various breeds and personalities thrown together in an unpredictable ecosystem. Among them was Eddie, a Dachshund. Short-legged, long-bodied, absurdly outsized by his canine counterparts. Yet despite his diminutive stature, Eddie possessed something far greater than muscle, he wielded attitude.

His greatest rival? Caesar, a German Shepherd four times Eddie's size. A dog who, by all rational measures, should have been able to crush Eddie in an instant. And yet, Caesar ranked at the bottom, forever trapped beneath Eddie's dominance.

The interaction was almost ritualistic. Caesar, eager for a meal, would wander toward the food bowl, oblivious to Eddie's watchful gaze. But Eddie never intervened immediately. No, that would lack impact. Instead, he would wait, calculating the perfect moment, allowing Caesar to settle into his meal before striking.

As soon as Eddie approached, Caesar stopped eating, his conditioned instincts kicking in. At the first sight of his Alpha, he froze, his body tensing in anticipation. Eddie, in contrast, rose to full height (as much height as a Dachshund can muster), ears erect, tail lifted, chest puffed. Then came the growl. The slow, deliberate baring of teeth.

Caesar responded by dropping his ears, tucking his tail, lowering his body, making himself smaller. He submitted, as he had countless times before. And Eddie, ever the tactician, refused to relent until Caesar had lowered himself sufficiently. Sometimes punctuating his dominance with a quick snap of the jaw, enough to make Caesar release a nervous trickle of urine.

It was comical. Entertaining. And yet, at its core, it was fascinating. Caesar, by all logic, should have overturned the hierarchy. Physically, he had every advantage. And yet, he didn't. Why? The answer, strangely enough, lies in chemistry.

No, not steroids or artificial enhancers, but the raw biological chemicals produced within. Hormones. Neurotransmitters. The invisible forces that dictate behaviour, perception, and dominance. And not just in dogs. In humans, too.

Neurochemistry and the Battle for Dominance

Ascending or descending within a dominance hierarchy triggers profound neurochemical shifts, altering motivation, aggression, and social behaviour. At the core of this battle are two key players: dopamine and octopamine, opposing forces that dictate confidence, submission, and survival strategies.

Those who thrive at the top, the Eddies of the world, are dopamine junkies. Dominance fuels them, driving them toward continual success, reinforcing their status-seeking behaviours. Studies on ants, for example, show that dominant individuals exhibit higher dopamine levels, correlating with reproductive success and greater aggression. Nature, in its ruthless efficiency, ensures that the strongest procreate, securing robust offspring and the continuation of the species.

In humans and other vertebrates, dopamine sharpens ambition, fuelling assertiveness and goal-oriented behaviour. The dominant constantly chases their next fix, small victories stacked upon one another, feeding an endless cycle of self-reinforcement. Eddie's food bowl ritual? A perfect illustration. Each time Caesar submitted, Eddie experienced chemical validation, reinforcing his instinct to exert control.

And Eddie didn't stop there. His dog-bed strategy mirrored his approach to the food bowl. Caesar, finally resting, minding his own business, would inevitably face Eddie's calculated aggression. Eddie would approach, slowly, deliberately, his posture rigid, ears pricked, tail lifted in silent authority. Caesar, conditioned by countless encounters, lowered himself instinctively, ears back, tail tucked, body shrinking in a futile attempt to appear less threatening. Sometimes, Eddie's dominance remained psychological, a mere display of superiority. But then, arrogance took hold. Power, when unchecked, seeks further expression. One day, Eddie, fully aware of Caesar's surrender, lifted his leg and marked him. A declaration, primal and indisputable, "You are mine, boy. To torture and dispatch as I see fit."

And thus, in that moment, dominance was not simply established, it was engraved into Caesar's psyche.

Octopamine: The Chemical of Submission

Where the Eddies bathe in dopamine, the Caesars are flooded with octopamine. A chemical often compared to noradrenaline in vertebrates, associated with stress responses and submissive behaviour. Studies in insects reveal that higher octopamine levels correlate with lower dominance status, driving behaviours of avoidance and withdrawal.

In hierarchical structures, both canine and human, those lacking dopamine exhibit hesitation, submissiveness, and a tendency to yield rather than fight. And here, the correlation is undeniable. Caesar, physically superior, had the raw power to reverse the hierarchy. But chemically, he was programmed to submit.

And so, the same biological forces that governed Eddie and Caesar govern us. Dopamine and octopamine shape human ambition, rivalry, and social interactions. Influencing emotions, perceptions of power, and even our willingness to challenge authority. It is why some people, despite intellect, talent, and capability, find themselves overshadowed by seemingly inferior individuals, not because they lack strength, but because they lack the chemical drive to assert it.

And here lies the deeper question: is dominance dictated by ability, or simply by chemical advantage?

For nature cares little for fairness. Only us humans dare dilute the natural order of things by entertaining equality and equity. Human rights and cordiality. It is not governed by moral philosophy, nor by sentimental ideals. It exists solely to ensure survival. Something us humans will have to come to terms with, when our survival as a species is threatened, it will be the result of our weakness. The lesser will be responsible for the destruction of the whole. Because the strong allowed the weak to dominate. And by strong, I refer to those that should be at the top of the dominance hierarchy, however, they have allowed themselves to be suppressed by mediocrity. Allowing the mediocre to rise to dominance. It is inevitable that the strong, intellectually, and in some cases physically superior, should dominate. Its is the way nature intended.

The Chemical Divide: Dopamine vs. Octopamine

The influence of dopamine and octopamine on both dogs and humans is profound, shaping not just mood and motivation but the very mechanics of dominance, submission, and survival strategies.

The dopamine-soaked elite, those who thrive at the top of the hierarchy, possess enhanced energy levels, sharper focus, and an insatiable appetite for risk. Their bodies are chemically primed for ambition, confidence, and assertiveness, reinforcing behaviours that secure their status and continued success. Meanwhile, the octopamine-flushed individuals, those resigned to submission, face heightened stress, anxiety, and diminished motivation, trapped in a biological cycle of avoidance and fear.

No wonder bullies seek to further intimidate the lesser, it is an easy dopamine fix, a self-reinforcing cycle that deepens their dominance while further weakening their victims.

Take Caesar, for example. Each time he stepped toward the food bowl, his body forced him to eat, yet his mind remained conditioned by King Eddie's ritualistic torment. He associated the food bowl with psychological defeat. Though necessary for survival, each meal became an act of submission, triggering a release of octopamine, a chemical warning that braced him for impending intimidation. Eddie, on the other hand, saw these moments as opportunities. For him, these encounters were not just acts of dominance, they were dopamine rushes, fuelling his sense of power, control, and well-being. Each successful display of authority strengthened his neurochemical reward loop, reinforcing his status and confidence.

Neurochemical shifts like these extend far beyond social interactions, they shape decision-making, behavioural patterns, and physical health. But as with any drug, prolonged exposure has biological consequences. Though octopamine temporarily stimulates adrenaline and norepinephrine, sharpening alertness and boosting energy, it is short-lived and comes at a steep cost. Studies suggest octopamine suppresses appetite and increases metabolism, which might seem beneficial in certain contexts. However, excess exposure drives individuals toward frailty, leading to weight loss, malnutrition, and constant physiological distress. A Caesar consumed by octopamine becomes sickly, deteriorated, permanently locked in flight mode, his heart rate heightened, his lifespan ultimately reduced by the unrelenting burden of stress.

Meanwhile, dopamine imbalances, whether too high or too low, are tied to conditions such as depression, schizophrenia, ADHD, and bipolar disorder. An overabundance of dopamine, though advantageous in dominance, carries risks, compulsive behaviours, gambling, substance abuse, and reckless risk-taking.

And here lies the crucial distinction between Eddie and Caesar, their biochemical composition dictates their fate. Dopamine fuels confidence, reward-seeking behaviour, and overall well-being. It sharpens decision-making, encourages calculated risk, and fosters deferred gratification, qualities that strengthen both mental and physical resilience.

But its reach extends far beyond social dominance, dopamine plays a pivotal role in movement coordination, with its deficiency linked to Parkinson's disease. It regulates blood pressure, cardiovascular function, appetite, digestion, and metabolic processes. It even interacts with the pituitary gland, influencing hormonal balance. Bottom line? The Eddies of the world are healthier, stronger, and chemically primed for success.

Their immune systems operate efficiently, their bodies recover faster, and their minds remain stable. They experience greater life satisfaction, improved cognitive processing, and an innate ability to attract mates, as physical health and strength remain evolutionary markers of desirability.

Where Caesar struggles, Eddie thrives, his dominance reinforced not by sheer force, but by the very chemicals nature has granted him.

Breaking the Cycle: Reclaiming Balance

The octopamine-flooded Caesars of the world live in a constant state of anxiety, desperation, and self-doubt. They scramble for scraps, settling for whatever they can get, unable to afford patience or selectivity. Their bodies betray them, manifesting the effects of prolonged stress, mangy fur, weakened immune systems, deteriorating health. Their every movement reflects caution, their tails low, ears drooping, eyes scanning for unseen threats.

Meanwhile, the dopamine-fuelled Eddies ascend, each success reinforcing their self-confidence, ambition, and dominance. Their victories multiply, feeding a cycle of reinforcement, spiralling them higher in status and authority. And like any powerful stimulant, dopamine becomes addictive, leading to the well-known phenomenon of being addicted to success.

But here's where the real danger lies, both Caesar and Eddie are locked into their cycles. Caesar sinks deeper, his octopamine levels stacking upon each setback. Eddie, in contrast, rises, his confidence expanding exponentially. Without intervention, Caesar is doomed to submission, while Eddie becomes increasingly reliant on dominance for his sense of fulfilment.

So how does one break the cycle?

Avoiding the False Fix: Why Drugs Make It Worse

One instinctive response to chronic low dopamine is seeking external chemical substitutes. Narcotics like crystal meth, heroin, and cocaine mimic the effects of dopamine, offering a short-lived sense of relief, masking the mental and physical strain of octopamine overload.

But this relief is an illusion.

Artificial dopamine does not bring the same cognitive and physiological benefits as naturally produced dopamine. Instead, it tricks the brain, briefly suppressing octopamine's distress signals, only for the inevitable crash to send the individual deeper into depression, desperation, and withdrawal.

Every drug-induced high lead to a stronger comedown, worsening stress levels and reinforcing the cycle of addiction. The next fix becomes urgent, feeding the very chemical imbalance that fuels octopamine dominance. This is why drug users exhibit the same symptoms as octopamine-flooded individuals, paranoia, impulsivity, withdrawal from society, increased anxiety, deteriorating physical health. Their survival instincts become warped, sacrificing relationships, stability, and even essentials like food and clothing, all in pursuit of the next artificial dopamine hit. Simply put, drugs do not break the cycle. They accelerate it.

They kill you, slowly and painfully, while convincing you they offer salvation.

The Real Solution: Rebuilding the Natural Dopamine Cycle

To turn the tide, one must cultivate natural dopamine, not through shortcuts, but by changing behavioural patterns. Yes, the shift from submissive to dominant is as easy as changing your mind and your actions. However, these should not just be actions, they should become habits. The first step in the process is a mental shift. Before changing what you do, you need to change why you do it. Seeing the glass half full, instead of half empty, will enable you to cultivate a mindset of appreciation, of thankfulness. Seeing the little things that are in your favour and appreciating them. Then use methods such as to start off by setting small, achievable goals. Goals that you achieve easily and then your mind will reward you with dopamine. This will create a positive loop. Repetitive iterations of success and reward will create a genuine reward-seeking behaviour. Compliment these efforts by engaging in physical activity to trigger natural dopamine release. Exercise. Building resilience through discipline, teaching the mind to associate effort with success. By fostering positive social interactions, reducing stress responses through camaraderie and bonding. With the emphasis on positive. The key is resetting the chemical hierarchy, shifting away from octopamine dominance and restoring dopamine-driven momentum. It requires effort, awareness, and deliberate action, but it works. Not only does it work, it will lengthen your lifespan and it is far cheaper than drugs. And unlike drugs, it builds strength, rather than disguising weakness. Drug users are weak. Lacking the fortitude to generate their own "well-done-juice" (dopamine).

The human brain, arguably the most sophisticated computer on the planet, is surprisingly easy to hack. And the first step? Realization. Caesar suffered not because of physical inferiority, but because of psychological blindness, an inability to recognize his own potential to dominate. His submission was not fate, but manipulation, tactfully executed by Eddie, reinforcing a cycle of self-doubt and restraint. Humans, however, hold a distinct advantage, the power of cognitive thought, the ability to evaluate our own actions, challenge our beliefs, and rewrite our behavioural programming.

The key to breaking the cycle? Success. Imagine a cognitively aware Caesar, determined to rewrite his fate. His first step: to establish a routine. Caesar chooses 6 AM as his wake-up time, Monday through Sunday, no exceptions. Each successful morning reinforces consistency, and with consistency comes accomplishment. Accomplishment = success. Success = dopamine.

Step two of Caesar's redemption: Physical conditioning. Though low energy, Caesar understands that exercise regulates blood pressure, strengthens resilience, and triggers dopamine release. Yesterday, he managed five push-ups, today, he pushes for seven. Success. More dopamine.

Caesar is already starting to feel better about himself and his circumstance. He moves to step three: Confidence in Posture. No more slouching, shoulders back, chest out, chin down (chin down is key; we seek confidence, not arrogance). The mind reacts to posture, reinforcing self-assurance with dopamine rewards. Caesar also know his mind listens to what comes out of his mouth, so in step four: verbal affirmations. When Susi the poodle casually greets him, asking, "Hey Caesar, how are you holding up?", he no longer defaults to weakness. Instead, he smiles and declares with conviction: "I'm doing well, better every day. Thanks for asking, Susi."

His brain listens, validating the statement with dopamine. And Susi? She senses confidence, she sees strength returning. Suddenly, Caesar is not invisible anymore.

See, success builds upon itself. The downward spiral of self-destruction flips into an upward spiral of self-improvement. Caesar is no longer anxious and impulsive. His energy increases. His digestive health stabilizes. His confidence strengthens. The cycle feeds itself, momentum turns into motivation, motivation into dominance.

And then, one day, Eddie approaches. Eddie being confident and riding the dopamine high. This time, Caesar does not shrink. This time, he growls back. This time, he bares his teeth. And when Eddie moves in to intimidate, Caesar pushes back, firm, unwavering, undeniable. The hierarchy has shifted. The system is hacked. And the German Shepherd rises. Strong and confident, as a German Sheppard should. The first to notice is Eddie, surprised and confused. He does not know what to do with the unfamiliar taste of defeat. It tastes like failure, like second place. It tastes like octopamine.

Mother nature rejoices, so too does the others whom have suffered under Eddie's rule. And so, begins Eddie's struggle for his rightful place on the ladder. He will have to fight, intimidate and manipulate for his position. The only fairness that nature offers, a fair chance at success.

Psychological Self-Défense: Breaking the Cycle

Too often, we allow ourselves to be trampled, just as Caesar was beneath King Eddie's ruthless rule. The manipulators rise, not always through merit or strength, but through tactful influence, subtle coercion, and psychological warfare. Politicians, managers, HOA dictators, even within families, the dynamics of power and submission play out endlessly.

But here's the unsettling truth: most manipulation is not intentional. People don't wake up plotting to extract dopamine by controlling others, it is subconscious, automatic, embedded in the very nature of social hierarchy. And now, as you reflect, you may even recognize instances where you yourself have engaged in subtle manipulation. No judgment, just awareness. The key is to recognize it, learn from it, and refuse to perpetuate the cycle of suppression.

We need to recognize the Eddies in our lives. Whether Eddie is a person or an institution. A boss, controlling and demanding. Having you do all the work and suppressing your career and opportunities for advancement. Or perhaps Eddie is a government. Selectively feeding the populous some information, just enough to make itself look good. Never enough to reveal its own inadequacies. Eddie might be hiding in plain sight, but because you have been blinded by your octopamine saturated existence, you have not realized it and not recognised Eddie. Eddie could be a competitor, dominating your industry. Relentlessly controlling the market, standards and the general narrative. It could be, that Eddie sleeps next to you at night. Calls you husband or wife. Slowly and methodically manipulating you into thinking it's your fault. Making you feel guilty for something. Systematically moulding and constructing the relationship into something very one-sided.

Assess your state of being. Use this book as a dopamine – octopamine thermometer. Stick it under your tongue and see what it says. If your octopamine level are high, ask yourself, through brutal and uncompromising honesty, whom or what is the cause of this. What makes you anxious and why? If you feel inadequate, who makes you feel this way? Determine the causes that attempts to push you down the happiness-ladder. Then scrutinise the motives. If you are uncertain of the motives, probe deeper.

This process requires objectivity. For only through impartial assessment, can you recognize the manipulator. Who knows, the manipulator might be staring back at you in the mirror.

In Jundokan, the international organization devoted to Okinawan Goju Ryu Karate, the dojo-kun serves as a guiding philosophy, a moral code recited at the close of every class, reminding practitioners of the values they uphold. One such principle states: "Do not be too proud, or modest." It is tied to the famous words of Chojun Miyagi Sensei, the founder of Goju Ryu: "Do not strike others, and do not allow yourself to be struck." And here, the lesson is clear: Do not manipulate others, and do not allow yourself to be manipulated. Learn the art of psychological self-defence. A powerful tool, one that demands self-awareness, resilience, and the ability to call out manipulation before it takes root.

Now bow, but stay sharp. Class is far from over.

The Mechanics of Manipulation

Manipulation, though difficult to define in singular terms, follows a structured psychological process, often used to control and influence others, sometimes consciously, sometimes unconsciously. At its core, manipulation employs several key strategies, systematically guiding behaviour, perception, and response to serve the manipulator's objectives.

The process could be broken down into six stages. Although this seems intentional and deliberate, unconscious or undeliberate manipulation follow the same process. At the beginning, the manipulator starts with observation and understanding. Before any real influence takes hold, the manipulator must assess their target, their emotional vulnerabilities, fears, desires, motivations. This step is foundational, shaping all subsequent tactics.

The manipulator has seen potential, now, he or she needs to establishing rapport. Once the manipulator understands their subject, they work to gain trust and familiarity. Often through mirroring (subtly copying physical, verbal, and emotional cues) or love-bombing (flooding their target with affection, validation, or generosity, only to withdraw later). Both tactics are highly effective in lowering defences. They are also very effective in negotiations and sales. I teach my students these techniques as part of their entrepreneurial studies.

Next, comes the process of exploiting the vulnerabilities. After establishing trust, the manipulator begins to steer their target toward a desired outcome, using emotional triggers like guilt, fear, flattery, or obligation to exert control. This is not isolated to weaknesses; vulnerabilities could be strengths too. If a person or group has untapped or unappreciated potential, this could provide the vulnerability required for manipulation. Political parties are a classic example of manipulators that exploit such.

To position the exploitation, the manipulator might distort reality. Perception itself is a tool, whether through gaslighting, misinformation, or selective truth, or outright lies, the manipulator subtly warps reality, making their target doubt their own judgments and lean on the manipulator for clarity.

The penultimate step is creating urgency & pressure. Once their grip tightens, the manipulator accelerates the decision-making process by inducing panic or time sensitivity. Peer pressure may also be leveraged, convincing the target that noncompliance would lead to consequences. Some might call upon the law, some might issue ludicrous, self-generated fines like the HOA's. Some might rally the support of your mother-in-law or perhaps even the children.

Finally comes reinforcement & continued control. Success reinforces the manipulation. Once a person submits, their behaviours are continually shaped and reinforced, ensuring prolonged control. Like the child in the mall. Repeatedly fortifying its tantrum driven control over mommy.

If you reflect on past interactions, you may recognize these tactics, either used on you or even employed by you (don't worry, your secret is safe with me). Again, I stress that these steps might be very subtle. To refer to an analogy used by a particular political party, it is like having frogs in a pot of water. Slowly the temperature rises and before the frogs realize it, it's too late.

Recognising the manipulator

The Dark Triad of Personality consists of Psychopathy, Narcissism, and Machiavellianism, three traits that, when combined, create individuals highly skilled in deception, influence, and manipulation. However, these traits are not exclusive to diagnosable individuals, they exist in varying degrees within all of us.

Psychopathy is generally characterized by the lack of empathy, prioritizing self-interest, and exhibiting impulsivity. They manipulate for pleasure and complete disregard for the consequences. In many cases, the consequence is what brings the pleasure.

Narcissism is the sense of inflated self-importance, the craving admiration, and leveraging charm. They lack accountability and manipulate to benefit and buttress their sense of prominence. It is important to note that all psychopaths are narcissistic, but not all narcissists are psychopathic.

Machiavellianism, they are identified by cold calculation, strategic manoeuvring, and relentless in their pursuit of control. While psychopathy and narcissism fall within clinical disorders, Machiavellianism remains purely strategic, inspiring many to study and refine the art of persuasion, influence, and cunning. And yes, many of the Machiavellian traits are desirable traits. Let me explain.

One of the most influential guides to Machiavellian strategy is Niccolò Machiavelli's The Prince, an ever-relevant blueprint for political and psychological dominance, illustrating the fundamental rules of manipulation and power acquisition. Because whether in politics, business, or social hierarchy, manipulation remains a survival tool, and those who master it wield an undeniable advantage. You too might want to research some of these traits and adopt some of these behaviours. Agility, perceptiveness and tact for example. Having these tools renders you no longer defenceless. A sovereign state with no military has no means of protecting itself. You can also not simply erect walls and shut out the world in fear of being manipulated. You cannot, because you struggle to play the game, quit and sit on the side-line. No, you are in it. In it to win it. Unless you wish to resolve yourself to being the Caesar, prior to his awakening. Doomed and destined to meet an early end. A victim of his own, self-induced incarceration behind the bars of octopamine.

The Subtle Art of Manipulation: How It Shapes Our World

Manipulation infiltrates social, professional, and personal interactions more deeply than most realize. Often disguised as persuasion, influence, or negotiation, it thrives on exploiting cognitive biases, those unconscious shortcuts our brains take when making decisions. Even those who believe themselves immune to manipulation, those who claim they'd never be hypnotized or coerced, are subject to the same psychological triggers that drive marketing, politics, law, and relationships.

Consider hypnosis, not the swinging pocket watch of Hollywood, but the real science of subconscious access. It is present in advertising, in the legal system, even in everyday conversation. Picture yourself driving down the highway, minding your own business, until a billboard disrupts your neutrality: A soda pouring into a frosty glass. Suddenly, thirst emerges where there was none. A steak sizzling on the grill, juicy, flavourful, hunger awakens instantly, triggered by nothing more than an image. You didn't choose to feel hunger or thirst, the subliminal messaging did it for you. And it doesn't stop there. Marketers hack your brain regularly and continuously. Seeking triggers and means to bypass your mental defences. People study, for years, the effects certain colours have on the mind, the optimal speed of a video advertisement, the best font to use in text. Leaders pay massive amounts of money for advisors to tell them what colour tie to wear to board meetings or media briefings.

Learn to recognise people motives and drivers. I teach the repetitive questioning process. If someone says A, ask why are they saying it. If the answer is because they seek help. Then ask why again, why are they seeking help. Continue the questioning until you reach the cause. The root. The driver. Questioning why, helps you look past the symptoms.

Helps you dig through the rubble that cover the cause. When you reach the source, examine it to be true and just. Is it in fact for the better?

Manipulation can be as subtle as word placement or sentence construct. Sometimes as simple as the act of a hand shake. A prominent President can repeatedly be observed shaking hands with dignitaries and counterparts. However, he has a unique habit of pulling the other person's hand toward himself when shaking hands. This is a gesture of dominance. The pulling of the hand, sets the other person up as "I am allowing myself to be pulled, manipulated." The pulling of the hand also sets the other party up by already putting the mind into giving mode. "I give my hand, my space, and I allow you to take." See just how subtle manipulation can be?

A courtroom attorney, seeking to guide a defendant toward a desired response, might frame questions strategically. Starting off with a harmless question, structured to naturally elicit a "yes". Then another simple agreement, reinforcing compliance. A third affirmation question is asked, priming the defendant's mind toward yes-mode. And then comes the critical fourth question, framed with precision: "Would you then agree that, although it was unfortunate that Mr. ABC died, you acted in anger when you pulled the trigger?" The likelihood of another "yes" is now statistically elevated, not by force, but by the careful engineering of language. The mental defences have been bypassed and the supercomputer has been hacked.

Marketers live by this principle, using precisely these techniques to close deals, drive engagement, and influence behaviour. I personally have used many of these techniques and others like it during negotiations and sales to much success.

You too, should learn to look past the obvious. Beyond what is on the surface and look deeper. People's intent is what drives their behaviour. If you probe, you will discover the intent and better be able to decide if you wish to go along with the suggestion or resist it. Eddie's intent was not to eat the food in the bowl, it was merely to intimidate Caesar.

Emotional Manipulation: The Currency of Relationships

The most intimate forms of manipulation unfold in relationships, woven into emotional blackmail, withdrawal tactics, guilt-inducing strategies. The closer you are to someone, the more they know about your habits, preferences and dislikes. It makes it easier for them to take advantage of this knowledge and the privileged position they find themselves in. In a relationship, you have already agreed to let the other party in beyond the public persona. You have voluntarily lowered your defences and exposed the private persona. Leaving you even more vulnerable than for instance at work. This is why most people are manipulated by close friends and their partners.

A partner sulks and withdraws when they don't get their way, forcing the other into compromise through guilt. Another plays the puppy-dog-eyes trick, filling their gaze with tears (that one always works), knowing emotional appeal overrides logic.

And the worst, withholding intimacy as leverage, cheapening what should be sacred into a mere transaction: "If you don't play golf, if you help more, if you avoid spending time with your mother, then, and only then, you'll be rewarded."

Such tactics may succeed in coercion, but they slowly erode trust, respect, and authenticity, turning something profound into mere barter. Don't be surprised if the other party one day finds an alternative source for what you have now commoditized.

Ah, now you see it.

Not just how manipulation surrounds you, but perhaps even how you've unconsciously wielded it yourself. It's uncomfortable, isn't it? That realization. That manipulation isn't exclusive to others, that we all engage in it, knowingly or not. You might not be good at it, so you deem yourself a victim thereof. But you most certainly have done it before yourself.

And that's precisely why this book exists. Not merely to expose others, but to unpack the manipulative tendencies within ourselves. After all, I didn't just study it.

I lived it. And the revelation was so profound, I wrote a book about it.

The Psychology of Influenceability

No matter how resilient or self-assured we believe ourselves to be, none of us are immune to influence. Manipulation is embedded within human nature, because connection and empathy, two fundamental aspects of social survival, also make us vulnerable to persuasion and coercion.

Influenceability is shaped by psychological, social, and environmental factors, all of which dictate how susceptible we are to external persuasion. For example, where we discussed in the previous chapter how letting one's guard down and getting close to someone does expose our psychological under-belly. But that does not mean you should never open up. It does not mean you should never trust anyone. On the contrary, this knowledge will enable you to better judge whom to trust. Then you can trust fully and wholeheartedly.

Let's examine some more traits of people, not the manipulators, but this time the manipulatees. Those susceptible to manipulation. Yes, we all are vulnerable. We are all unique, just like everyone else. (Did you get that?) However, there are some that are more susceptible than others. So let us look at the key traits that make people more influenceable.

Openness to new Ideas should be self-explanatory. Those who are naturally curious and open-minded are often more receptive to persuasion, as they actively seek new perspectives and possibilities. They are openly inviting new concepts and foreign influence. Talk about vulnerability, wow.

Then there are the emotional sensitivity people. Highly empathetic or emotionally driven individuals may be more easily swayed by compelling narratives, as they internalize external emotions rather than maintain emotional detachment. They are subjective thinkers and are quick to put themselves "in the other person's shoes". That is an easy way to also get someone "on your side". Being the side of the manipulator.

One big vulnerability is insecurity and need for social acceptance. Those who crave approval or seek belonging often conform to group norms or influential figures. Just think of the innocent virtuous girl, seeking approval and validation. Then the prom date uses the phrase, "But if you love me, you will...." Happened all too often. Manipulation 101.

Children with low self-confidence frequently submit to peer pressure the same as adults with low self-esteem tend to follow authoritative personalities, often without question. They thrive on the authority of others.

Through exposure to persuasive communication is something society nowadays have a huge challenge with. Prolonged engagement with marketing, media rhetoric, and political messaging can gradually shape thought patterns, especially when information is selectively presented to control narratives. As is the case on social media. Yet we allow our children almost limitless access to social media and accept them following INFLUENCERS. Influencers might as well be call manipulators. In most cases they simply push some sort of narrative and often that narrative is not a healthy one.

That brings us to the deep psychology of conformity. Something that manipulators use to manipulate masses, not just individuals.

Humans, by nature, prefer not to stand out, especially when placed in a strange environment, surrounded by unfamiliar individuals. When faced with high novelty and social uncertainty, we seek safety in conformity, often abandoning independent judgment to blend in with the group.

A fascinating ethical question. Can a normal person with strong values be manipulated into committing atrocity, willingly? This is a question I ask my students as part of their studies on marketing. History, and psychology, suggests yes, it is absolutely possible. But how?

From groupthink experiments to real-world historical events, manipulation through social pressure, authority figures, and normalization has led individuals, who otherwise would never harm another person, into acting against their own moral compass.

As an entrepreneur, I teach students the principles of persuasion, demonstrating how even something seemingly impossible (selling ice to an Eskimo) can be achieved through strategic influence. But beyond business, this same psychology applies to conformity in more extreme circumstances.

Think about situations where individuals conform, despite knowing something is morally wrong.

Now, let's examine real-world examples where this theory was put to the test, and what the results revealed about human psychology.

In the early 1960's Milgram devised an experiment to test if it was in fact possible to get a normal, good person, to do terrible things, conducted at Yale University. This study aimed to measure obedience to authority by instructing participants to administer electric shocks to a "learner" whenever they answered incorrectly. Participants were told they were taking part in a study on memory and learning. The shocks were fake, but the participants believed they were real. The test subject was placed in a room in front of a panel of buttons. The buttons were clearly marked in increasing levels of voltage. From 15 volts through to 450 volts. From the 250-volt button upwards, was clearly marked "POTENTIALLY LETHAL". The "learner" was placed in another room and supposedly strapped to a chair with electrical wires attached in a way that would provide electric shock whenever the buttons are pushed. Each time the 'teacher' would ask a question and the learner responded with an incorrect answer, the test subject was instructed to press the button that would deliver the electric shock to the learner. With each incorrect answer, the voltage would increase. This would trigger screams of pain and agony over the speakers where the test subject could hear it. The screams were pre-recorded and not real, but the test subject had no way of knowing this. The test subjects were encouraged through "the experiment requires that you continue" and "It is absolutely essential that you continue".

Before the experiment, they predicted that perhaps one out of a hundred test subjects would in fact venture as far as the potentially lethal dose of 250 volts. Indicative of some psychopathic tendencies. But with all the test subjects being of various backgrounds but generally common, everyday Joe Soaps, it was more than likely that nobody would risk potentially electrocuting another human being.

Care to venture a prediction of your own? What do you think? Would you have gone as far as pressing that button marked potentially lethal, while listening to what could possibly be the learner's last screams of terror?

The results were astonishing. Not only did 100% of the test subjects go all the way to 250 volts, but Milgram found that 65% of participants obeyed instructions to administer the highest voltage of 450 volts, despite hearing the learner's distress. Most participants showed visible signs of stress, hesitation, and discomfort, but still followed orders. The presence of an authority figure greatly influenced participants' willingness to obey, even when it conflicted with their morals.

The Milgram experiment stands as one of the most unsettling yet illuminating studies in human psychology. The prediction, that only a tiny fraction would go beyond the 250-volt mark, was quickly dismantled by reality. The results were shocking (both figuratively and scientifically). In the original study, 65% of participants pressed the maximum 450-volt button, fully believing they were inflicting deadly pain on another person. They obeyed, not because they were cruel, but because authority told them to.

The essence of this experiment isn't about whether a person is good or evil, it is about the power of authority and the terrifying ease with which obedience overrides morality. Under the right circumstances, ordinary individuals, fathers, mothers, teachers, can be guided into actions they would otherwise deem unthinkable. They are not heartless, they are conditioned to trust authoritative figures, believing that responsibility for harm lies elsewhere. And this is exactly why we should take great care with whom exerts authority over our children. Whom the teachers are. For the last thing you want is for some dilutional teacher, abusing their position of authority, to manipulate your child into conforming. Nor should we tolerate the government dictating and manipulating the truth through selective exclusion of scientific, biological and even historical facts.

Would you have pressed the button? That is the question that lingers. Many would confidently say "No, absolutely not", until placed in the heat of the moment, under social pressure, authority directives, and incremental justification. Would the fear of disobeying outweigh the horror of harming another? History suggests... probably yes.

And that is the lesson Milgram left us with, evil does not require malice, merely blind obedience.

If Milgram's experiment exposed the ease with which people abandon morality in the face of authority, then the equal line test reveals how social pressure alone can override objective reality.

An experiment was conducted to see if the test subjects would conform to the group, even if it means they would provide and answer they know to be untrue. A group of ten subjects were placed in a room. Nine of the ten were all in on the experiment and number ten was the true test subject. The group was shown two pictures. The first had three lines of different length on it. Marked A, B and C. The second page had only one line, marked D. The group was asked to choose based on visual evaluation, which one between A, B or C is equal in length to D. The nine group members that were in on the experiment were briefed beforehand to purposefully give the incorrect answer. They all said B, even though C was clearly the same length as D. When it came to the tenth person, the true test subject, it was found that the vast majority of them would also go with the rest of the group in selecting B, even while they know C to be the correct answer. Again, the test subjects would go against what they know to be the truth, for the sake of conforming. Not standing out.

The results? Even without direct coercion, the test subjects conformed, deliberately selecting the incorrect answer, despite knowing it was wrong. Why? Because standing apart, even when correct, can feel more uncomfortable than blending into collective error.

This experiment highlights the core mechanics of influence. We do not want to appear different and we do not always want to stand out. This is due to our fear of isolation. Subconsciously we desire to belong and this overrides the logic of independent reasoning. There is also the added complexity of perceived majority wisdom. If everyone else believes B to be correct, then maybe I am missing something. Maybe I am wrong. And that invokes the avoidance of social discomfort aspect. Where we would rather conform because confronting others demands confidence, risk-taking, and a willingness to endure scrutiny. And we more often than not, do not possess the appetite for such when it comes to strangers. And this principle applies far beyond a simple test of line length.

It explains corporate cultures, where employees remain silent in the face of unethical behaviour. It explains political movements, where individuals echo narratives, they may personally doubt. It explains war crimes, where soldiers follow orders rather than challenge morality.

It proves, once again, that manipulation is not always forceful, it is often silent and subtle. It is very often self-imposed. Like Caesar. And that, perhaps, is the most dangerous form of control, the silent pull of social influence.

The Brain Games experiment takes manipulation one step further, proving that obedience isn't required for influence to take hold, sometimes, mere observation is enough. No orders, no coercion, no explanations, just behaviour repeated often enough that it becomes accepted without question.

This experiment tested whether individuals would follow group behaviour without understanding the reason behind it. The setup was where a waiting room was filled with actors, who were aware of the experiment. A woman, the first test subject, entered the room for what she believed was a routine appointment. Everyone was sitting quietly reading or scrolling through social media on their mobile devises. Every time a buzzer sounded, the actors stood up and sat down without explanation or demonstrating anything else other than, this is how it should be. Nobody spoke or coerced the test subject to also stand when the buzzer sounded, they simply stood and sat down again. Initially confused, the woman observed the behaviour. By the third beep, she joined in, standing up and sitting down with the group. As the experiment progressed, all the original actors were called away, leaving only the woman. Despite being alone, she continued standing at each beep. New participants entered the room, saw her behaviour, and eventually followed suit, without knowing the original reason.

This experiment demonstrated social conformity, where individuals adopt behaviours simply because others around them do. It highlights how people often follow group norms without questioning them, reinforcing the idea that social influence can shape behaviour even in the absence of logical reasoning. How the individuals and even a multitude can be manipulated into following a certain idea or action without knowing its cause, motive or reason. We humans are so easily manipulated.

The test subject didn't need a reason to stand and sit, she simply followed because the group did. And as new participants entered, they too followed, further solidifying the absurd ritual into an unchallenged norm. Manipulation Without Force: The Power of Silent Conditioning. This experiment reinforces an uncomfortable reality: Humans tend to mirror social behaviour, even when it lacks logic. We do not always question the validity of collective actions; we assume the group must know best. And influence often requires no persuasion, only repetition and observation. AS is available on social media. One could watch the same TikTok over and over. Plus, the same message can come in various forms and dressed up as different faces.

It's the same mechanism behind cultural traditions, corporate norms, political ideologies, and daily societal expectations. It begs the question; how much of our lives are shaped by unexamined conformity?

The degree to which someone is susceptible to manipulation, their influenceability, can be measured and observed through psychological assessments, behavioural tendencies, and social dynamics. As inherently social beings, humans rely on collective validation, whether consciously or subconsciously, making us vulnerable to external persuasion.

There are multiple factors that determine manipulability. People with an external locus of control, those who consistently seek validation from external sources, whether through peers, authority figures, or social approval, are more easily subjected to manipulation. They depend on external opinions to define their worth, making them highly influenceable.

People that are prone to openness & agreeability, are individuals who are naturally open-minded and agreeable tend to assume others share their sincerity, making them prime targets for exploitation. Their desire for harmony can be leveraged by those who lack the same ethical restraint.

Neuroticism and overanxious behaviour also render one very vulnerable. Those prone to obsession, excessive worry, or emotional instability are easier to manipulate, as appealing to their sensitivities, even superficially, can override rational defences.

Cognitive reflection ability is something that psychologists test using a Cognitive Reflection Test (CRT). Its purpose is to evaluate how critically an individual processes information before accepting it. Those who blindly trust messages without analysing intent are more likely to fall prey to manipulative tactics.

The Danger of Unnoticed Manipulation

What makes manipulation particularly insidious is that it is often subtle, unrecognized, and wielded by those closest to us. We may only realize we've been manipulated in retrospect, long after behavioural patterns have been shaped.

Your insight into superficiality and materialism, especially within younger generations, aligns perfectly with this conversation. When self-worth is dictated by possessions rather than character, susceptibility to external influence skyrockets. The pressure to norm, to fit in at any cost, overrides individual authenticity, making manipulation effortless for those who exploit social expectations.

With today's hyper-connected digital landscape, the speed of influence is unprecedented. Trends explode overnight, news spreads like wildfire, and we've engineered an entire profession, 'influencers', whose sole purpose is to alter public perception. Artificial intelligence algorithms track search history, time spent on content, and engagement rates, then tailor ads to match observed interests. Targeted marketing ensures high-success persuasion, using data-driven psychology rather than direct coercion. Manipulation in marketing is no different from persuasion, convincing consumers to part with money for carefully marketed products.

Why Does This Matter? If you work in marketing, leadership, or politics, this knowledge is critical, knowing how manipulatable someone is determining how effectively you can influence them. And now, as you reflect, perhaps you see how you yourself have been manipulated, or even how you have unknowingly influenced others.

Simply put, the easier someone is swayed, convinced, or coerced into changing their perspective, the more manipulatable they are. If you rate yourself high on manipulability, we should certainly assess methods to defend against it.

Avoiding Manipulation & Mastering Influence

Manipulation is neither inherently good nor inherently evil, it is a tool, and like any tool, its impact depends on the intent behind its use. The ability to influence effectively is a skill worth mastering, not for deception, but for self-preservation, leadership, and navigating complex social structures.

Jordan Peterson's insight, "You need to be a monster, then learn to control it." rings true in the realm of manipulation. Rather the warrior in the garden than the gardener in the war.

To effectively resist manipulation, you must first understand how it works. Once you recognize its tactics, you will more quickly identify manipulators in real time, shielding yourself against them.

Machiavellianism has been described as the "blueprint for strategic influence". Niccolò Machiavelli's philosophy revolved around power, strategy, and calculated influence. Manipulation, in Machiavellian terms, is not impulsive deception but long-term orchestration, a measured approach toward control and advantage. High-Machs (those with strong Machiavellian tendencies) exhibit traits that would include the prioritization of strategy over ethics. Their focus is on results, not moral concerns. Often leaving a mess of collateral damage in their wake. They strive towards and very often achieve mastery of deception and persuasion. They use charm, subtle coercion, and social leverage to shape outcomes. Whatever it takes. Using different strategies for different targets. Their emotional detachment enables them to resolve themselves, then end justifies the means. They view relationships transactionally, avoiding deep emotional ties that compromise their long-term plans. Often leaving then lonely and more focused on their strategies than on meaningful, fulfilling partnerships. And do not be fooled, thinking short term. Oh no, these guys and girls are in it for the long haul. Long-term manipulation, unlike short-term deceivers. High-Machs strategize for months, even years, moving players across the board like a chess grandmaster. Chess games that could span over decades.

Understanding Machiavellian traits allows you to identify manipulators before they strike. Learn to read intent, not just actions, but the motivations behind them. Watch for things like charm used for personal advantage. Not all charming individuals manipulate, but those who consistently leverage charm for influence often do. Look out for distrustful people. Manipulators rarely trust others because they assume everyone else is as strategic as they are (A spy sees spies everywhere). Also be cautious of avoidance of deep connections. Those who thrive on surface-level relationships, dodging commitment or emotional vulnerability, often use people as tools rather than companions.

Interrogate intent before you engage. If something feels off, ask questions. Manipulators rely on trust and lack of scrutiny, the less they are challenged, the more freely they operate. And if you have been manipulated before, recognize that learning from the past is a shield, not a cage. You don't need to shut the world out, but move cautiously, test loyalty, and allow yourself to open up selectively. (Yes, I am talking to you. Yes you.)

By understanding how and why people manipulate and more importantly developing the ability to spot manipulation, you will save yourself much pain, embarrassment and loss. To use another analogy, it's a tough world out there and you can decide if you want to be a wolf (not all wolves are evil), or a sheep. There was an instance somewhere in Europe where one sheep jumped off a cliff. The others, being sheep, followed. Hundreds of sheep leaped from the cliff in a senseless and callous act of blind assimilation. Needless to say, the ones that went first all died a horrible and abrupt death. Majority survived, since there was instead of the hard, rocky earth, a softer woolly pile of corpses that cushioned their fall. We don't have the luxury of trusting that there might be something or someone that would cushion our fall. Rather be a wolf. Sheep graze blissfully unaware of things happening around them. The probability that a sheep will notice a wolf in time for it to still make its escape when attacked, is very low. So instead of going through life with an oblivious, trust-fuelled and sheepish (see, what I did there) attitude, you should become more aware of what people do and why. Developing your ability to avoid becoming the victim of manipulation. It is how you protect yourself. It is how you shed your wool and become a wolf. How you become the monster. Then, you can choose to be a vegetarian wolf, if eating sheep does not sit well with your values. At least you will be a wolf. And this is what is required. Having the ability to be ferocious, savage and merciless, in your pursuit for truth, happiness and honesty. Intolerant of manipulators and untouchable by their devious tactics.

Machiavellian traits, often associated with manipulation and self-serving tactics, are not inherently negative. In fact, when applied with ethical intent, they can be powerful tools for leadership, negotiation, and decision-making.

The key distinction lies in intent, when aligned with the greater good, strategic influence can drive efficiency, innovation, and success. But when weaponized for deceit, it undermines trust and integrity. Machiavellianism in leadership and business strategy can be very effective and beneficial. High-Mach leaders make cold, pragmatic choices, prioritizing long-term vision over sentimentality. While harsh, this approach often ensures success in environments where emotional considerations can hinder objectivity. The best Machiavellian minds read social structures expertly, allowing them to steer decisions, maintain authority, and create advantageous conditions. However, withholding or distorting information crosses into unethical manipulation, this distinction must be respected. High-Machs also form strong partnerships to advance shared goals but are keenly aware when an alliance loses value. Learning when to withdraw and when to strengthen connections is a crucial skill, one that prevents exploitation.

Another trait that will be beneficial to acquire, would be the Machiavellian's ability to outmanoeuvre competitors by anticipating moves and countering them with strategic planning. Perceptiveness. My kids used to get so frustrated with me when at the start of the movie, I would identify the villain, only to have my prediction validated by the end of the movie. They never could understand how I managed to do that. It's a combination of situational awareness and perceptiveness. A technique used by mentalists all the time.

Negotiation is not just business contracts, it is woven into daily interactions, relationships, and decision-making. We continually negotiate, with our partner, our friends, at work. A marriage proposal, family planning, or social commitment are all negotiations, requiring persuasion and strategic thinking. Being good at negotiations is a pivotal competency. For we speak not just verbally, but through body language, tone, gestures, and even scent. Yes scent. Hormones, pheromones, all of these are detected and communicates state of health, maturity, virility, and much more. Words do not always align with posture or expression, the ability to spot inconsistencies is essential.

Successful negotiators, especially those with Machiavellian skill, master persuasion, adaptability, and calculated risk-taking. But ethical influence must always override deception, using manipulation for mutual benefit, rather than exploitation, secures trust and lasting success.

We have laid out a compelling case for perceptiveness, not just as a tactical advantage, but as a shield against manipulation. It's the ability to anticipate, observe, and counter, much like a strategist manoeuvring on the battlefield or a mentalist reading subconscious cues.

Situational awareness, as we have demonstrated is a skill worth honing. It allows you to see patterns, detect inconsistencies, and predict outcomes before they unfold. And when applied to social interactions, it becomes a powerful defence mechanism against deception.

While Machiavellianism excels in efficiency and strategic planning, it is a double-edged sword. Without ethical oversight, it can lead to manipulative relationships, distrust, and a lack of transparency. The best leaders understand this balance, strategic thinking without compromising integrity, long-term success without deception.

It's about knowing how the game is played, but choosing when and how to engage, ensuring your influence remains grounded in truth rather than coercion.

The sheep, content in blissful ignorance, move with the herd, unquestioning, unaware of looming threats.

The wolf, by contrast, analyses, adapts, and anticipates, not always as a predator, but as a survivor. Wolves are monsters. They devour sheep for breakfast. But being a monster and having the capabilities of a wolf, does not have to be used on sheep. It could and should be a defensive mechanism. Being the wolf. But having the tendencies of a wolf under control. Basically, you should become a vegetarian wolf. The embodiment of the ability to be ruthless, when necessary, but restrained by conscious choice. Not about destruction, it's about self-preservation, discernment, and mastery over influence. The goal is not just to detect manipulation, but to build resilience, counter deceit, and control one's own strategic capabilities. It is ferocity in the pursuit of truth. To be untouchable by deception. The refusal to be prey. Cultivate awareness without losing integrity.

This, perhaps, is the true path to power, not manipulation for its own sake, but influence wielded with intent and responsibility.

Conclusion

If you've made it this far, you've not only gained insight into how manipulation works, but you've also learned how to recognize it, counter it, and even harness it for ethical influence.

Manipulation, whether intentional or unconscious, is woven into daily interactions, leadership structures, and societal norms. But true strength lies in the ability to see through illusions, reject mediocrity, and act with purpose and conviction. This isn't just about identifying manipulators, it's about refining your own influence, ensuring you remain untouchable by deception while mastering the art of persuasion. Manipulators aren't limited to politicians or corporate leaders; they exist in every corner of life.

They sit in boardrooms, shaping narratives. They whisper in friendships, steering decisions. They operate in families, bending relationships to their will.

And sometimes, if we're brutally honest, they exist within ourselves.

Because at some point, we've all manipulated, whether subtly or overtly. Awareness isn't about rejecting influence altogether, it's about choosing when, how, and why to wield it.

The world is ruthless, it demands resilience, adaptability, and strategic thinking. You can choose to be the prey, like Caesar, or be the one who sees through the games and plays them better.

So, sharpen your mind. Strengthen your awareness. And take control. Because the best strategist is never the one being played, but the one holding the board.

Now go get them, tiger.

Don't miss out!

Visit the website below and you can sign up to receive emails whenever Morne Fourie publishes a new book. There's no charge and no obligation.

https://books2read.com/r/B-A-XNUOE-GUZJH

BOOKS 2 READ

Connecting independent readers to independent writers.

About the Author

Morne Fourie is a South African author, strategist, project manager, and entrepreneur, whose work bridges the realms of emotional sovereignty, leadership philosophy, and innovation. With a doctorate-in-progress, Fourie brings a rare synthesis of academic rigor, psychological insight, and visionary pragmatism to every page.

His *Personal Insight Series* distills decades of inquiry into human behavior, influence, and resilience. Drawing from monastic traditions, ancient and modern philosophy, neuropsychological frameworks, and lived experience. Whether modeling scalable business systems or crafting emotionally resonant fiction, Fourie's voice remains unwaveringly committed to clarity, autonomy, and ethical impact.

A master of layered storytelling and strategic design, he has led ventures in energy solutions, manufacturing, mergers, acquisitions, and divestments of various enterprises, always with an eye toward sovereignty—personal, communal, and infrastructural. His business acumen is complemented by his study of psychology and human behavior. His writing honors the dignity of suffering and the possibility of healing, offering readers not just insight, but transformation.

Through this series, Fourie invites readers into a space of remembrance and recalibration: where solitude becomes strength, structure becomes sanctuary, and insight becomes a tool for grace.

www.ingramcontent.com/pod-product-compliance
Lightning Source LLC
LaVergne TN
LVHW022311200926
848481LV00004B/1276